A Noisy Day for Meow Meow!

Written by **Felix Cheong**

Illustrated by
Yunita Elvira Anisa
& Devitha Fauzie

mc **Marshall Cavendish**
Children

I hear a singalong song in my sleep.

"Good morning! Have you caught your worm yet?

You must have had your fill, I bet!"

What is that? Soft and loud, all around,

my home is awake with many sounds.

Hear that hiss? Here, put your ear on this wall.

And I sneak in to stop Mummy's snore!

Clink, clang, clickety clack.
What sound can smell as good as that?

Pancakes and eggs, pots and pans,
Breakfast is in Mummy's good hands.

Wah, wah, wah! Baby runs here and there.

But Daddy puts her in her feeding chair.

I hear a low grumble, a grr, grr, growl.

My empty tummy seeks out my dish and wow.

Crisp fresh crackers! Crunch and crackle,

As I crouch in my happy corner.

Pitter-patter, pelting on the pane, then boom!

I duck under the bed in my room.

Whooo. Whooo is that calling outside our door?

Whoosh, it must be the wind sweeping the corridor.

"Looks like we cannot go out in this rain,"
Daddy says as mmmmmmm, something goes off again.

I am just happy for Baby's company

As the boom, boom, boom fades slowly.

Just when I get a little sleepy,

another big noise comes at me.

Whirrrrr! With a long tail, it rolls on wheels.

This noisy day will not end, I feel!

Tick-tick, tick-tick. When I open my eyes,

A beaming sun greets me in the sky.

All is quiet now, at least for a while,

Till everyone comes home with a wide smile.

About the Author

Felix Cheong is the author of 21 books.
Conferred the Young Artist Award in 2000 by the
National Arts Council, he works as a university lecturer.
This is his seventh children's picture book.

About the Illustrators

Yunita Elvira Anisa is an illustrator based in New York City
who specialises in ink and water-colour work. Her focus is
botanical subjects and natural landscapes.

Devitha Fauzie is a designer and illustrator based
in Jakarta. She has been interested in art from a
young age and studied art at tertiary level where she
encountered digital art. Since then, digital painting
has been her passion and medium of choice.

Published by Marshall Cavendish Children
An imprint of Marshall Cavendish International

A member of the
Times Publishing Group

Other Marshall Cavendish Offices:
Marshall Cavendish Corporation, 800 Westchester Ave, Suite N-641, Rye Brook, NY 10573, USA ● Marshall Cavendish International (Thailand) Co Ltd, 253 Asoke, 16th Floor, Sukhumvit 21 Road, Klongtoey Nua, Wattana, Bangkok 10110, Thailand ● Marshall Cavendish (Malaysia) Sdn Bhd, Times Subang, Lot 46, Subang Hi-Tech Industrial Park, Batu Tiga, 40000 Shah Alam, Selangor Darul Ehsan, Malaysia

Marshall Cavendish is a registered trademark of Times Publishing Limited

National Library Board, Singapore Cataloguing-in-Publication Data

Name(s): Cheong, Felix. | Anisa, Yunita Elvira , illustrator. | Fauzie, Devitha , illustrator.
Title: A noisy day for Meow Meow! / ‡c written by Felix Cheong ; illustrated by Yunita Elvira Anisa & Devitha Fauzie.
Description: Singapore : Marshall Cavendish Children, [2022]
Identifier(s): ISBN 978-981-4974-91-2 (paperback)
Subject(s): LCSH: Cats--Juvenile fiction. | Household sounds--Juvenile fiction.
Classification: DDC 428.6--dc23

Printed in Singapore